D1281382

DREAM IT
TO DO IT

Praise for *Dream It to Do It: The Science & the Magic*

"Drawing upon ancient wisdom and contemporary
scientific discoveries, Eisenberg asks his readers to
take a daring plunge into a different way of perceiving
the world than what they have been taught."

—STANLEY KRIPPNER, Ph.D., California Institute of Integral Studies, California

"… the book is AMAZING!!! I love it!!! It reflects in a such
clear way, who we are, and how our consciousness works in this
multidimensional world. I felt 100% reflected and finally someone
was able to put in writing what I feel so strongly. On another
note the list of recommended online resources is fantastic."

—CARLOS DAVIDOVICH M.D., Neuromanagement Consultant, Spain

"Delightfully pithy and wise book."

—DEAN RADIN, Ph.D., Chief Scientist, Institute of Noetic Sciences, California

"I'm amazed at how you communicated so much content,
so eloquently and so efficiently."

—CLAUDIA WELSS, Chairman, Board of Directors, Institute of
Noetic Sciences, California

"…this book provides profound insights into
the nature of mind and reality…"

—DAVID LORIMER, Programme Director of The Scientific and
Medical Network, *Paradigm Explorer*

"…takes a deep dive into exploring the nature of reality
and the evidence for the primacy of consciousness in
an upbeat guide for the psychically adventurous."

—PARAPSYCHOLOGICAL ASSOCIATION, *Mindfield Bulletin*

DECODING REALITY 2.0

DREAM IT
— to —
DO IT

The Science & the Magic

HOWARD EISENBERG, M.D.
FOREWORD BY STANLEY KRIPPNER, PH.D.

ALSO BY HOWARD EISENBERG

Inner Spaces: Parapsychological Explorations
of the Mind (Musson, 1977)

Les Espaces Intérieurs (Le Jour, 1981)

Espacios Interiores (Editorial Posada, 1983)

تأليف هاوارد إيزنبرغ ؛ ترجمة الحارث عبد
الحميد، أسيل عبد الرزاق ؛ المراجعة اللغوية،
عبد الأمير الأعسم (Bayt al-Ḥikmah, 2001)

CONTENTS

FOREWORD
Stanley Krippner, Ph.D.

In 1977, Dr. Howard Eisenberg published *Inner Spaces,* a pioneering book that enabled its readers to apply the findings of parapsychological research to their daily lives. His current book greatly expands the scope, providing ways in which people can use their imagination to envision better lives. Not only does he review centuries of pertinent philosophical and scientific literature, additionally he outlines specific methods and procedures by which his readers can implement the shamanic adage of "dreaming their world into existence."

Underlying these processes is the provocative contention that consciousness is not the by-product of one's brain and body, but is fundamental to all of existence. Just as the universe is constantly awakening to itself, individuals can rouse themselves from their culturally imposed beliefs, their conditioned habits, and lifestyles that they automatically follow without reflection, awareness, and critical thinking. The philosopher Alan Watts urged his audiences to go beyond their "skin-encapsulated egos" to transcend their society's limitations. Another philosopher, George Gurdjieff, attempted to rouse people from their "waking trance." Both philosophers provided exercises to "awaken" to the greater reality, and Eisenberg follows in this tradition.

Drawing upon ancient wisdom and contemporary scientific discoveries, Eisenberg asks his readers to take a daring plunge into a different way of perceiving the world than what they have been taught. But for what purpose? The inhabitants of contemporary civilizations are marked by discontent, massive depression, and catastrophes of their own making. Eisenberg is well aware that we are living in critical times and his book is a valiant effort to turn the tide. His suggestions are thoughtful—but they are also practical. They are based on connection, community, and love. It is my fervent hope that they are widely considered and practised; if so, this short book will have massive effects for a world badly in need of healing and redirection.

Stanley Krippner, Ph.D., is currently Associated Distinguished Faculty at the California Institute of Integral Studies. He is an internationally eminent psychologist, parapsychologist, and author of several hundred research papers and multiple books on altered states of consciousness, shamanism, and parapsychology. He is a recipient of the American Psychological Association's Award for Distinguished Contributions to the International Advancement of Psychology.

Reality is merely an illusion, albeit a very persistent one.

—Albert Einstein

Whatever you can do, or dream you can do, begin it. Boldness has genius, power, and magic in it. Begin it now.

—Goethe

AUTHOR'S NOTE

This is a massive update of my groundbreaking book *Inner Spaces: Parapsychological Explorations of the Mind*, which was published back in 1977.

I was called to write this book, at this time, as a critically needed wake-up call to you all because these are *very dark times* with multiple existential threats.

Since childhood, I've been on a passionate mission to explore *how reality works*. Along the way, I've had the good fortune to meet internationally with enlightened scientists, philosophers, spiritual teachers, visionaries, healers, and psychics. I have also been a *psychonaut*, personally exploring altered states of consciousness to experience *the plasticity of conventional reality*.

Welcome now to my deep dive into exploring the nature of reality. In the pages that follow, you will learn about the overwhelming evidence of the *world-behind-the-world* and the *proof* for the primacy of consciousness. More importantly, you will learn about our true nature and the innate *magical resources* that are our birthright but often forgotten about in our technology-dependent modern world. It is my sincere hope that this is the beginning of a journey for you, one in which you will begin to tap into these resources to create a happier, more satisfying life, as well as a safer and healthier world.

This is not an ordinary book. It's designed to be read slower (much slower) so you can reflect very deeply and actually experience an expansion of your consciousness!

ACKNOWLEDGMENTS

I have been an eager lifelong student of these subjects. Along the way I've had the opportunity to learn from and personally meet many wise and admirable teachers from diverse backgrounds. I have also read many books and journal articles by outstanding scholars and scientists that have helped shape my own thinking. I simply connected the dots to see and convey the bigger picture.

This book is a composite of my learnings from multiple sources—too many to properly reference them all. I therefore appreciatively dedicate this book to all my true fellow scholars and scientists.

Know thyself.

—Oracle of Delphi

Seek, and ye shall find.

—Matthew 7:7

01

Things Are Not as They Seem

Imagine

how radically different your experience and understanding of reality would be if you were born in primitive times, before the development of our modern technologies.

Even in our current era, there are many different prejudices, ideologies, and religions—all immersed in the same reality but with very different interpretations and beliefs.

We're programmed by our experiences to see reality through different lenses. Our beliefs are like filters, blinding us to how others might see and value things very differently.

However, if you're willing to examine and challenge these limiting beliefs, you can discover who you really are—and could be—instead of being restricted to what you have been taught to believe, or how you're treated by others.

> *For things to reveal themselves to us, we need to be ready to abandon our views about them.*
>
> —Thich Nhat Hanh, Vietnamese Buddhist monk and global spiritual leader

It takes courage to explore what really is, to be open to seriously questioning what you believe to be true—especially if it doesn't align with what you were previously led to believe (or the views of others around you).

On the other hand, can you really buy in to the prevailing scientific belief that you're just a type of machine made of meat, that your sense of self is merely an illusion computed by your brain, and that you live in a meaningless universe?

What if our sense of reality, and even the existence of the physical brain itself, despite convincing appearances, is no more fixed and "out there" than our nightly dreams?

Many of the spiritual teachers of the world conceive of us as being asleep, failing to realize that we're just caught up in our dreams. They teach that the *egoic self* with which we identify is what keeps us emotionally entrapped in this virtual, but all-embracing, illusory world.

Things Are Not as They Seem

Even apparently solid material objects are not solid, but mostly empty space. Yet we can see and touch them, despite their ghostly reality.

Perception Changes Reality

In the martial arts of karate and taekwondo, young children are taught to break through wooden boards with their bare hands by imagining that they are forcefully thrusting *through and beyond* the board, rather than hitting it. Similarly, there is the altered-reality experience of people walking unharmed while barefooted over extremely hot coals—as long as they *believe* they can do so without being burned.

Your perceptions are not based on an objective external world, though they do provide a very convincing simulation of such a virtual reality out there.

As we become entrapped in our interpretations of reality, our emotional attachments and fears restrictively condition our future actions. The Buddha realized that we need to *let go* of our limiting beliefs about who and what we are, as they are the cause of unnecessary suffering.

If you're willing to risk going beyond the familiar comfort of your programmed limiting beliefs, then you can learn to do some *real* magic.

Qigong is an Asian form of yoga that has been practiced for thousands of years. The advanced practitioners of this craft are able to intentionally imagine projecting their internal vital *Shen* energy outward, either as a force for distance-healing or as a defensive weapon against an aggressor.

The sophisticated Russian martial art of *Systema* stems from a hybrid of the fighting techniques of the militaristic Cossacks and the Asian martial arts. It was developed for modern military use by experts within the Russian Special Forces. Advanced practitioners like Colonel Mikhail Ryabko have been observed physically impacting people positioned several feet away—with only their trained force of mind.

In both Qigong and Systema, advanced practitioners use the imaginal power of their minds to project an outward influence on the plasticity of conventional physical reality. They purposely imagine the desired energetic feelings and intended impact so as to manifest them in the outer world.

And, according to leading-edge research at the Institute of Noetic Sciences (IONS), which was established by American former lunar astronaut Edgar Mitchell, something is in fact generated when talented subjects in experiments intentionally *imagine* influencing highly sophisticated technological devices that are physically and electromagnetically shielded.

Hmm . . . maybe you're not just a "skin-encapsulated ego."

Before we delve more deeply into this subject, first we need to attend to our existential predicament on the more mundane level of our consensual reality.

> *The situation the Earth is in today has been created by unmindful production and unmindful consumption. We consume to forget our worries and our anxieties. Tranquilizing ourselves with overconsumption is not the way.*
>
> —Thich Nhat Hanh

The untamed *egoic self* has a delusional and inflated sense of who and what it thinks it is. It emotionally hijacks our mind to compel us toward behaviors that are self-serving and shortsighted, often at the expense of others. It's constantly on the lookout for external rewards in an unrelenting need for still more and more to compete and validate its worth. It dismissively dehumanizes others. The result is our tribalistic us-versus-them conflict-seeking mindset—and the exploitation and pollution of our planetary resources.

Enlightened human behavior, by contrast, stems from a sense of connection with others and is characterized by compassion and collaboration. Ironically, this is also self-serving, according to the Stress Theory founder Dr. Hans Selye. As Selye discovered, one of the best biological protections against excessive stress is the development of an altruistic ego, an awareness and compassion for the needs of others. In other words, when we are more *connected* with each other, we are happier and healthier.

Various cultures have a creation myth like the Garden of Eden about a time of abundance and harmony before humans lost their connection to our spiritual source.

In the legends of the subsequent fall from grace, our ancestors came to mistakenly believe that their inner well-being depended on external material resources. The meaningfulness of life was sacrificed to the altar of material consumerism, and the spiritual-like aspects of nature, with its awe-inspiring grandeur and innate harmony, became desacralized into mere commodities to be exploited.

> *If people see how we're all interconnected and connected with Nature, we wouldn't have an environmental crisis and we wouldn't have wars all over the world.*
>
> —Stanley Krippner, psychologist and parapsychologist

Traditional aboriginal values were founded upon honoring and conserving nature and all other sentient beings. The Iroquois are believed to have codified this stewardship perspective in their Great Law as the Principle of Seven Generations. This was the wisdom to think ahead to help the world be sustainable seven generations into the future, as opposed to humanity's present shortsighted obsession with fears and greed.

The abandonment of the traditional aboriginal values coupled with the rise of our predatory-exploitative mindset has culminated in the current existential crises for humanity and our planet. It has endangered the entire web of life and is leading us to the point of human extinction.

Now is a critical time for all of us to wake up from the dystopian world we've created through blind acceptance of the spiritually eviscerated, materialistic view of reality. A world reality where, according to the World Health Organization, depression is the leading cause of disability. The landmark report released in 2018 by the UN Intergovernmental Panel on Climate Change (IPCC) concluded that there were only twelve years left to limit the impending global climate change catastrophe. The Doomsday Clock has been maintained by the Bulletin of the Atomic Scientists since 1947. It's a symbolic tracking system representing the probability of humanmade global catastrophes (such as from nuclear conflict, global climate change, pandemic mismanagement, and artificial intelligence). Reflecting multiple existential threats, the Doomsday Clock has been steadily inching toward doom since 2010, but as of 2021, for the first time, the clock's setting had to be expressed at the critical level of just one hundred seconds to midnight.

As Barbara Marx Hubbard, the late American futurist, author, and speaker, pointed out, "We are the first species who faces extinction by its own acts and knows it."

As then-sixteen-year-old climate activist Greta Thunberg expressed more angrily in her 2019 speech to the United Nations:

> People are suffering. People are dying. Entire ecosystems are collapsing. We are in the beginning of a mass extinction and all you can talk about is money and fairy tales of eternal economic growth. How dare you! . . .
>
> We will not let you get away with this. Right here, right now is where we draw the line. The world is waking up and change is coming, whether you like it or not.

The COVID-19 pandemic, with its lack of adequate vaccines for the poor and less developed countries, and the ongoing generation of even more potent viral mutations, exemplifies our need to think globally. As stated by UNHCR (the UN Refugee Agency), "No one is safe, until everyone is safe."

Ironically, in this modern era of scientific wonders, the very information technologies and social media platforms that connect us instantaneously are also responsible for separating us from *feeling connected*. This is because in spite of some seductive features, IT only connects us in the superficial horizontal dimension, as opposed to the deeper and more satisfying vertical dimension. This has resulted in increasing complaints of loneliness and even the appointment in the UK and Japan of ministers of loneliness to their governments.

Despite the current dim trajectory we find ourselves on, we all—each and every one of us—has a choice. We can continue to be defined by our past and play a fatalistic character in humanity's gradually unwinding story or we can be *Dreamers of the Dream,* intentionally generating new and more desirable experiences.

And, as you will soon learn, there is power in your dreams. By transforming your personal dream, you can participate in seeding a new and better vision for the world.

The Butterfly Dream

Once upon a time, I dreamt I was flying as a butterfly. However, soon I awakened and was my familiar self again. Now, I do not know whether I was then a man dreaming I was a butterfly, or whether I am now a butterfly, dreaming I am a man.

—Master Chuang-Tzu, fourth-century BC
Chinese Taoist philosopher

Ye shall know the truth, and the truth shall set you free.

—John 8:32

02

The Only
Thing You Can
Absolutely Know

I've frequently posed a variation of *The Butterfly Dream* to my many students and colleagues over the years. I challenged them to prove beyond any doubt that they were not, in that very moment, merely dreaming. Not one of them over those many years could solve this fundamental challenge. The implications of this thought experiment alone are rather staggering—because if you can't be certain whether or not you're dreaming, then there's no certainty about the very existence of a shared external reality.

Our perception of the world does have the very convincing appearance of being externally out there around us, but in reality it is no more out there than are our fantasies and dreams.

The Vedantic philosophers of India referred to this misinterpretation of illusion as *Maya*.

Consider the ancient parable *The Blind Men and the Elephant* from the Indian subcontinent. It's the story of a group of blind men who have never previously encountered an elephant. They learn to understand the features of the elephant by touching it, but each of the blind men feels a different part of the elephant's body, such as the trunk, tusks, legs, and tail. They then describe the elephant based on their limited experience and get into conflict with each other because their descriptions of the elephant are, of course, different. The moral of the parable is that we just *assume* that others can plainly see and understand things as we do.

Similarly, Greek philosopher Plato's *Allegory of the Cave* is a wise parable about how sensory perception and belief are inherently subjective and therefore not the ways to discover absolute reality. The story is about a group of long-time prisoners inside a cave shackled to the wall. All they see are flickering shadows on the walls. One of the prisoners eventually escapes. Upon emerging from the cave, he is temporarily blinded by the brightness of the external sunlight. Eventually his vision adapts and he sees the beauty of the external real world. He returns to the cave to share his discovery and to liberate the other prisoners. However, on reentering the cave he is again temporarily blinded, this time by the absence of light before his eyes readjust to the interior darkness. The other prisoners perceive him initially as handicapped by his adventure and subsequently are too fearful to trust him and leave their familiar cave. They remain trapped, not by any material restraint but as prisoners of their fears and false beliefs.

The puzzle of *The Butterfly Dream* remains just as challenging now in our modern technological times. The more refined challenge to our common-sense understanding of reality was posed by the French philosopher Descartes in 1637 as a thought experiment. Aside from the question of being able to distinguish between dream reality and external reality, he posed an even more profound question to himself.

Descartes wondered what, if anything, could he absolutely know to be true, regardless of whether or not he was dreaming. And he came to the famous realization that he could doubt everything—except that he was doubting. He famously expressed this insight as "I think, therefore I am" (*Cogito, ergo sum*).

In other words, the *only* thing we can possibly know to be true is that we are experiencing *awareness of being aware* as our present reality (whether it be in a dream or an altered state of consciousness).

Further self-reflective observations are fundamentally restricted, as taught by Shankara, the eighth-century Vedantist, because the *Knower cannot know Itself.* In other words, the observer is not the same as that which can be observed (just like the eye cannot see itself or the tongue taste itself).

> *Our world only exists because we perceive it and act as conscious agents. Thus, all interactions with the universe are experiential and subjective.*
>
> —Menas Kafatos, physicist

We can only be certain of our personal conscious awareness.

Consider, then, at least the theoretical possibility that you've actually been living in a mind-generated, all-embracing collective illusion since your earliest childhood.

> *Most people think we believe our experience. This is not true; we experience what we believe.*
>
> —Sandra Ingerman, author on Shamanism

Ironically, Western materialistic science was developed to advance knowledge by examining only external, objective things, which could be predictably observed and measured, in contrast to people's subjective feelings and thoughts. However, as you will learn with amazement in chapter 5, as scientific discoveries in physics advanced, the apparent external material reality quite literally lost substance.

Of all the fads and foibles in the long history of human credulity, scientism in all its varied guises—from fanciful cosmology to evolutionary epistemology and ethics— seems among the more dangerous, both because it pretends to be something very different from what it really is and because it has been accorded widespread and uncritical adherence.
. . . One longs for a new Enlightenment to puncture the pretensions of this latest superstition.

—Austin L. Hughes, biologist, *The New Atlantis*, 2012

Imagination is more important than knowledge. For knowledge is limited, whereas imagination embraces the entire world.

—Albert Einstein, physicist and Nobel laureate

03

The Real Basis of Scientific Discovery and Invention

In prescientific times, the prevailing Western world-view, according to the Catholic Church and its interpretation of the Bible, was that Earth was the center of the universe and the sun and stars revolve around it rather than our planet being one of many others orbiting the sun. To even suggest otherwise was condemned as heresy.

But scientists Copernicus and Galileo challenged the Catholic Church's worldview with their discovery that our planet, Earth, is not only the center of the universe, but in fact just another of several other planets orbiting the sun.

For his crime of perceiving reality differently, Galileo was tried and convicted by the Inquisition in 1633. Interestingly, most of his closed-minded critics refused to even try to take a peek through the telescope at the sky above for themselves. Such is blind faith.

There's a masked successor of faith-based religion in our modern age—the promotion of scientific materialism. This is the unquestioned assumption that science is the only truthful way of gaining knowledge about reality and that everything in the world could be eventually explained in physical terms (i.e., *scientism*). Since the seventeenth century scientific materialism has increasingly become the dominant paradigm, with the resulting current existential threats (because, like the preceding religions, it's based dogmatically on an incomplete model of reality).

It was indeed progress to awaken from a passive, faith-based understanding of reality and to instead question everything in a reflective way. But is the logical scientific method really the process that has enabled our fundamental material discoveries and technological achievements?

What if less thinking equals greater consciousness?

Actually, all humanmade constructions and technological products in our external world were first created in the human imagination. Everything!

Contrary to popular belief, the major scientific discoveries were not the results of the linear, step-by-step "scientific method" of research, but rather emerged from mental imagination and intuitive feelings.

Nineteenth-century chemist and inventor Dmitri Ivanovich Mendeleev's development of the "periodic table of elements" provided a comprehensive system for classifying all the various chemical elements that make up the material world. It remains the basis of modern chemistry. (His chart even allotted spaces for elements that he anticipated but were yet to be discovered. For some of these missing elements, he was additionally able to predict their probable atomic masses and other chemical properties.) However, the basis for this breakthrough classification was simply his dream of watching it unfold before his eyes in his imagination. Mendeleev had previously tried all sorts of arrangements without success. One day, exhausted, he dozed off to sleep and had a breakthrough dream. "I saw in a dream, a table where all the elements fell into place as required. Awakening, I immediately wrote it down on a piece of paper."

German organic chemist August Kekulé also lived in the nineteenth century. Kekulé was trying to discover the arrangement of the carbon atoms that comprise the molecular structure of benzene. Like Mendeleev, he had long struggled without success. One night he dreamed of snakes rolling down a hill while swallowing their own tails. He awoke with a eureka insight. He realized that this crazy dream provided a symbolic representation of the ring-shaped molecular structure of benzene. Subsequently, this discovery became the basis of our seemingly essential modern petrochemical and pharmaceutical industries. But the inspiration came from his dream.

Albert Einstein engaged in his earliest, and most famous, thought experiment when he was just sixteen years old. He imagined himself somehow chasing after a beam of light. This played a key role in the eventual development of his famous "theory of special relativity" and many other still-foundational concepts in cosmology and physics. But it came about from his playful imagination.

Nikola Tesla's inventions are the building blocks for almost all our modern technology of electrical systems and devices. However, the key ingredient in his prolific career as an inventor was his power of *visualization*. Tesla first imagined and designed his inventions in his mind's eye. He could even visualize operating simulations, which then served as his guide to physically constructing them.

Alchemy has morphed and still thrives in our modern technological era, as exemplified by the plethora of clever apps for smart phones. The software programmers imagine the desired benefits and then manifest them into physical reality by writing the appropriate underlying computer code.

In addition to dreams and daydreaming, other altered states of consciousness yield incredible discoveries and achievements. One example is the "state of flow," a natural altered state of consciousness discovered by psychologist Mihaly Csikszentmihalyi. In this state, people like athletes and creative types are hyperfocused, feel energized, and are enjoyably immersed in their athletic or mental activities. In other words, people feel their best while also achieving breakthrough performance. Yet brain monitoring reveals that the most evolved and supposedly complex thinking portion of the human brain, the prefrontal cortex, is actually partly offline at such times (known as *transient hypofrontality*). Therefore, the optimal state of well-being and performance experienced in flow is not the result of our brains thinking smarter.

Psychedelic chemicals like LSD bypass the brain processing networks associated with our conventional perception and thinking (*entropic effect*). Yet some of the most impactful scientific developments in our modern physical world were the result of the super-enhanced imagination brought about by psychedelics-facilitated altered states of consciousness.

Nobel laureate Francis Crick, who envisioned the double helix shape of DNA, was both a consumer of and public advocate for mind-expanding substances. Another Nobel laureate, Kary Mullis, openly attributed his experiences with LSD to his subsequent discovery of the polymerase chain reaction (PCR), which enabled the modification of inheritance by genetic engineering and revolutionized the field of biology.

Before inventing the Apple computer and many subsequent revolutionary devices, Steve Jobs, the visionary genius of IT, first lubricated his mind by altering his consciousness with meditation and LSD.

Historically, some of the most consequential Silicon Valley computer engineers benefited from using LSD to enable them to design increasingly complex three-dimensional computer chips. Currently, microdosing with LSD is not uncommon among the IT workers out there for increasing their creativity (and lowering their stress).

(It should be noted, however, that careless personal experimentation with psychedelics can be like playing with fire: it can drive some people insane.)

So, in contrast with the popular assumption, the formula for breakthrough scientific progress is not the methodical scientific method of research, but bypassing the thinking brain.

Apparently, less brainwork equals greater consciousness.

And as for what we call reality—*it's from the inside out.* Imagination is the source of everything that we've developed.

Although the content of consciousness depends in large measure on neuronal activity, awareness itself does not. … To me, it seems more and more reasonable to suggest that the mind may be a distinct and different essence.

—Wilder Penfield, neurosurgeon and groundbreaking researcher

I maintain that the human mystery is incredibly demeaned by scientific reductionism, with its claim in promissory materialism to account eventually for all of the spiritual world in terms of patterns of neuronal activity. This belief must be classed as a superstition. … We have to recognize that we are spiritual beings with souls existing in a spiritual world as well as material beings with bodies and brains existing in a material world.

—Sir John C. Eccles, neurophysiologist and Nobel laureate

04

Brain Science and Consciousness?

As you learned in the preceding chapters, the only thing you can be certain about is your personal conscious awareness, at this moment.

Modern neuroscience would have us believe that consciousness is just an emergent epiphenomena resulting from the underlying complexity of the physical structure and processes in the brain. It's a huge assumption to believe that mental events are caused by physical events in the brain yet have no causal power upon the physical world. The so-called evidence is based on modifying the structure or processes of the brain and then observing any resulting changes in awareness and/or behavior. But correlation from association does not necessarily imply causation. And there is no evidence at all that the brain is the source of our experience of subjective consciousness.

There is not even a generally accepted theory of how the material brain could possibly produce our experience of consciousness. This is why the philosopher David Chalmers termed it the "Hard Problem."

New Age author Peter Russell cleverly reversed the materialist challenge: "How can something as immaterial as consciousness arise from something as unconscious as matter?"

Perhaps the brain relates to our experience of consciousness, but not its source. Consider a device such as a TV or smartphone, which can receive, display, and modify information. Physically damaging such a device can distort the display of the desired information. That doesn't mean, however, that the information is originating inside the device rather than being received from an external source:

a television station or other internet users. If the TV, computer, or network connections break down, other such devices can still access the same information. Reception is not the same as generation.

It appears that the brain serves more like a transducer device for consciousness, filtering and selectively processing downloads from consciousness. (Just as a radio or TV can be tuned to a variety of different broadcast stations, so can the brain tune in to different types of awareness.) And, as you will be learning, the brain also enables intentional uploads to consciousness as well.

Historically, the Greek-derived word *psyche* meant the underlying soul, or spirit. Ironically, psychology, the modern field of science specialized to study the workings of our minds, became sidetracked. Consequently, psychology became degraded into a secondary soft science. As cleverly ridiculed by the American psychologist Robert S. Woodworth: "First psychology lost its Soul, then its Mind, and then its consciousness."

Psychiatry has also become increasingly dismissive of the vital importance of attending to the deeper psyche, or inner spiritual self. Yet most comparative research studies of the various techniques of psychotherapy have found that the key critical factor for a successful treatment outcome was the experience of empathic connection between the patient and the therapist. The bottom line is that the relationship, not the techniques, is most helpful. Recently, there was an unusually loud wake-up call from Dr. David Rosmarin of Harvard's prestigious Department of Psychiatry. His article, published in the June 15, 2021, issue of *Scientific American,* is boldly titled "Psychiatry Needs to Get Right with God." It documents the research findings that support spirituality as a critically neglected aspect of proper mental health care.

We're born into an edited-reality version of the experiential world. What we can see, hear, smell, taste, and feel is not in fact the real world as it is but a virtual version that our brains process into our subjective perceptions.

Famed psychologist D.O. Hebb described the phenomenon of infants born with congenital cataracts who later received corrective surgery. Though the procedures were successful, the children could not meaningfully distinguish distinct figures (which they technically could now see properly) from an amorphous mass. They had to be taught first to "see" what they were *supposed* to. This is one of many psychological research studies proving that we don't see things as they are; rather, we see things as we are taught and *learn* to see them.

We also see the world through the lenses of our personal histories because our processed brain perception creates our realities. This is illustrated in brain-monitoring research on underlying racial and ideological biases. Researchers discovered that we subconsciously filter the same information but in different brain regions according to our core beliefs (i.e., *confirmation bias*). That's why simply presenting factual and logical information is not sufficient to overcome the emotionally conditioned ideological beliefs and prejudices of others.

What you experience is real—real to you. But it's an illusion to believe that you are aware of all reality rather than a processed and narrow bandwidth version. (Just as it was an illusion and an erroneous conclusion for the many who once believed that Earth was flat rather than round or that the universe orbited Earth.)

Thoughts Become Things

Not only does the brain not generate consciousness, but, on the contrary, brain research has revealed that intentionally changing how we think about things (such as by modifying personal habits or gaining insights through psychother-apy) has a physical impact on rewiring the brain (known as *neuroplasticity*). Consciousness can change both the physical hardware and software of the brain.

Psychoneuroimmunology is a relatively new field of medi-cine dedicated to researching how the mind can modify the functioning of the immunological system. It adds scientific validity to the old folk-medicine traditions for treating con-ditions such as skin warts, the modern day placebo effect, and unexplained "spontaneous" remissions from critical diseases such as cancer.

Epigenetics refers to the recently discovered ability of humans to modify our genes for our offspring. Meditation itself can cause relatively immediate changes in the poten-tial on/off functioning in the *gene expression* of more than a hundred genes involved in energy metabolism and inflam-mation (as demonstrated by Dr. Herbert Benson's research team at the Benson-Henry Institute for Mind/Body Medicine).

It's more like mind over matter.

Additionally, there are the experiences of nonordinary states of expanded consciousness in deficient brain conditions such as in hypoxia (insufficient oxygen for normal brain functioning), savant syndrome (genius-like abilities emerging from damaged brain structures), NDEs (near-death spiritual experiences with subsequent recovery, such as after resuscitation from cardiac arrest), and terminal lucidity (the experience of some cognitively-impaired people becoming clearheaded just prior to death).

Recently there has been some fascinating neuroimaging research with psychedelic substances such as LSD and psilocybin. These enable some people to experience a greatly expanded scope of consciousness with potentially transformative life impact. Yet although psychedelics are mind-expanding, many, if not all, such as psilocybin, actually reduce blood flow and neural activity in key brain centers (such as the large-scale default mode network comprising multiple important brain processing regions, including the most complex portion for higher-level executive thinking, the prefrontal cortex).

(However, as I previously cautioned—careless personal experimentation with psychedelics can also be unsafe, like playing with fire.)

Bottom line: it appears that less brainwork equals greater consciousness.

Adding to the controversy about the real relationship between the brain and consciousness is the medical discovery that our thoughts and emotions don't just happen in our heads. Science has discovered that we have at least two other physical brains—the heart and the gut microbiome.

Dr. J. Andrew Armour and his research team at the University of Montreal found that the heart has its own internal nervous system and is capable of storing memories. (This may explain the numerous medical reports of the transfer of heart donors' personality characteristics to their recipients.)

The heart also has more nerves extending up to modulate brain function than there are nerves extending down from the brain to modify cardiac activity. And it generates its own electromagnetic field, which is sixty times greater than the amplitude from the head brain. (The heart also secretes as much of the love-bonding hormone oxytocin as the head brain.)

The HeartMath Institute has additionally discovered that the heart plays a key role in accessing intuition. According to their research, it's connected to a field of information not bound by the classical limits of time and space.

Maybe there's some wisdom in the adage "Follow your heart."

Don't you generally prefer to interact with warm-hearted people, who are more authentic and caring?

The good news is that we can all choose to become more *heart-centered* to better access the heart's unique benefits. We can do this by shifting our bodily awareness from our head to our chest area and then tuning in to the subtle energetic changes within the heart area as thoughts and events occur.

The gut microbiome consists of trillions of bacteria

living in our large intestine, greatly outnumbering our human cells and total DNA. Interestingly, although they are bacteria, they are beneficial, symbiotic with our bodies. They play a vital role in helping to regulate the underlying physiological processes to sustain our health.

These bacterial organisms are necessary for the proper development of the head brain (such as myelination of the prefrontal cortex, which enables our complex thinking abilities and synaptic growth for neuroplastic upgrading). They also secrete their own neurotransmitters, such as serotonin, dopamine, and GABA, which modify the activity of our head brains for thinking, mood, and memory. Despite the current popularity of SSRI antidepressant medications for modifying the levels of serotonin in the brain, it's the microbiome in our guts that is the natural source of about ninety percent of the total serotonin in the body. Consequently, some psychiatrists are now prescribing targeted probiotics to enhance the microbiome for better gut health, along with psychotherapy.

Hmmm . . . maybe there is also some wisdom in the common expression *Go with your gut*.

In summary, although you are the user of your brain, you are not your physical brain—just as you experience and use your body, but you are not your body. As you will soon learn, you are potentially so much more.

In the beginner's mind there are many possibilities, but in the expert's, there are few.

—Shunryu Suzuki, Sōtō Zen monk and teacher

What is reality? The more we look at it, the less real it seems.

—*New Scientist*, February 2020

05

The Reality Challenge from the Discoveries of Modern Physics

Weirdly, the leading-edge scientific discoveries of modern physics about the nature of the external physical world increasingly correspond with the descriptions of the ancient wisdom traditions. Physics has to rely on complex high-tech equipment for its "discoveries." By contrast, the source for the ancient wisdom traditions was simply the subjective experiences of mystics. And yet soft mysticism and hard science are converging—ancient and modern, subjective and objective—on the same conceptions about the underlying nature of reality.

In the ancient and universal mystical conceptions of the world, which were based on subjective mental experiences, consciousness was considered central, and everything was interconnected.

Western science, by contrast, has long relied on speculation from the pre-Socratic Greek philosopher Democritus that ultimately everything is composed of different arrangements of separate fundamental physical atomic particles spread out through empty space. This conception that the true nature of things could ultimately be explained in material terms became entrenched in our modern era as the *materialistic-reductionist paradigm* of reality.

Democritus was partly correct in his speculation: there is an underlying atomic level of reality, as has been confirmed by modern physicists.

However, as we now know, atoms are over 99.9999 percent empty space. And it gets a lot more complicated and surrealistic, as we have further discovered.

The subatomic realm is freaky with particles that seemingly pop out of nowhere and at times appear more like waves than discrete things.

The atomic particles actually exist in waves of probability. It's the act of human observation that triggers the "collapse of the wave" into a particular material state. So the fundamental hard particles are based on speculation and probable outcomes (which I term *conceptrons*). It requires the act of human observation to condense a specific state of the probabilities down into material reality.

> *The universe does not exist "out there," independent of us. We are inescapably involved in bringing about that which appears to be happening. We are not only observers. We are participators. In some strange sense, this is a participatory universe.*
>
> —John A. Wheeler, eminent theoretical physicist

Then there's the quantum phenomena of "entanglement" and "nonlocality," which are the inexplicable instantaneous interconnectedness, without any intermediary, of otherwise distantly separate and disconnected atomic particles. In other words, things that affect other things at a distance without any explanation beyond that reality supposedly works that way. Einstein referred to this as "spooky action at a distance." The implications are that everything in the universe is both interconnected and interdependent.

In both the cosmologists' Big Bang theory and modern physicists' Quantum Mechanics, there is no need for an original creation story; they simply accept that the universe is and always has been.

It's also impossible to construct the fundamental explanatory theories in physics, such as quantum field theory, without relying on immaterial probability waves, "virtual particles," and ultimately highly sophisticated mathematics. Interestingly, those complex mathematics also depend on *presumptions*. (This includes so-called imaginary numbers—square root of a negative number—that doesn't have a tangible value like a real number that could be quantified on the number line but is nevertheless used in complex mathematical formulations.)

Moreover, the mathematician Kurt Gödel proved with his Incompleteness Theorem that mathematics can never be complete and therefore cannot be applied to fully model the universe.

So why do we experience things as being solid? The martial arts teacher and New Age explorer Lee Holden explains it with an interesting analogy: a spinning fan. When the fan rotates quickly, its blades visually blend together into an apparent solid. But when the fan is slowed down or stopped, the empty spaces between the blades become visible.

Ironically, materialism is but a metaphysical assumption. (And the physicists' universe is ultimately made out of "no thing"—nothing.)

Matter is conceived by the mind, rather than the mind being the product, or result, of complex physical brain processes.

The modern discoveries in physics are increasingly convergent with the ancient Hindu concept of the *veil of Maya*. This is the notion that what we perceive to be reality is only an illusion, albeit, as Einstein noted, a very captivating virtual reality.

For example, read the shocking conclusions from the most respected physicists of our modern era.

> *The notion of a separate organism is clearly an abstraction, as is also its boundary. Underlying all this is unbroken wholeness even though our civilization has developed in such a way as to strongly emphasize the separation into parts.*

—David Bohm, considered one of the most significant theoretical physicists of the twentieth century

> *. . . quantum physics teaches us that, in a very real sense, we all live in an imaginary reality.*

—Neil Turok, physicist and cosmologist

The universe looks more and more like a great thought, rather than a great machine.

—James Jeans, physicist and cosmologist

. . . the stuff of the world is mind stuff.

—Sir Arthur Eddington, astronomer, physicist, mathematician, and philosopher

I regard consciousness as fundamental, matter is derivative from consciousness. We cannot get behind consciousness. Everything that we talk about, everything that we regard as existing, postulates consciousness. There is no matter as such; it exists only by virtue of a force bringing the particle to vibration and holding it together in a minute solar system; we must assume behind this force the existence of a conscious and intelligent mind. The mind is the matrix of all matter.

—Max Planck, Nobel laureate physicist, famed originator of modern quantum theory

So our reality, the world in which we appear to live, is actually a constructed *consensual reality*. We are conditioned into accepting this version of reality by what we are taught and the pressures to socially conform. (Recall in the preceding chapter the research studies by psychologist D.O. Hebb on infants born with congenital cataracts who, after corrective surgery, had to be taught to see the world as "normal vision" people do. And then there's the research findings on the Whorfian Hypothesis, about how people in different cultures perceive and think differently because of the filtering differences in their languages.)

I am not one of those who dismiss a priori the study of so-called occult psychic phenomena as unscientific, discreditable or even as dangerous. If I were at the beginning rather than at the end of a scientific career, as I am today, I might possibly choose just this field of research, in spite of all difficulties.

—Sigmund Freud

The data in support of precognition and possibly other related phenomena are quite strong statistically, and would be widely accepted if they pertained to something more mundane. Yet, most scientists reject the possible reality of these abilities without ever looking at data! … Now there is a definition of pseudoscience—basing conclusions on belief, rather than data!

—Jessica Utts, 2016 Presidential Address to the American Statistical Association

06

Parapsychological Research on Mind Over Matter

Parapsychology is the scientific study of psychic phenomena (technically termed *psi*) that defy space and time and cannot be explained within the framework of the materialistic-reductionist view of reality. It's the branch of science that most directly studies the independence of consciousness from the physical brain and any other constraints of the material world.

Because I covered this subject in detail in *Inner Spaces: Parapsychological Explorations of the Mind*, I won't repeat it here. Suffice it to share that I have found from my own psychic experiences and extensive research that psi phenomena are not impossible and in fact do occur in many people from all walks of life.

I will also reveal a personal note from the early 1970s. At that time, at McGill University in Montreal, I pioneered the first postgraduate university degree in Canada for my research on telepathy. The chairman of the Psychology Department back then was internationally renowned Professor Donald O. Hebb (the American Psychological Association's journal *American Psychologist* cited him as one of the twentieth century's most eminent and influential theorists in the realm of brain function and behavior). But this esteemed scientist had gone on record in 1951 as dismissing all research results in parapsychology as being a priori impossible: "Personally, I do not accept ESP for a moment, because it does not make sense. My external criteria, both of physics and physiology, say that ESP is not a fact despite the behavioral evidence that has been reported. I cannot see what other basis my colleagues have for rejecting it . . . my own rejection . . . is—in the literal sense—prejudice."

Being idealistic and undeterred by Hebb's prejudiced viewpoint, I decided to apply to do my research in his department. This also ensured that it would have to be conducted under the tightest research conditions to overcome any possible skeptics.

Ironically, Professor Hebb's personal secretary typed my master's thesis detailing my successful experimental proof of telepathy. I happened to be in her office one day to collaborate on the final type-proofing when Professor Hebb walked out of his adjacent office. She saw him and excitedly called out, "Professor Hebb, you were wrong! ESP is real—this research proves it!"

Shortly thereafter he publicly recanted:

> ESP constitutes a problem for the good reason that all our present knowledge of the physical world and of the physiology of the human body make telepathy extremely unlikely and clairvoyance impossible, but at the same time there are certain experiences that seem to admit of no other explanation. There is also a body of experimental reports to support the latter view. The result is a difficult choice if we are to lay any claim to consistency of thought. Either the experimental data are untrustworthy and those apparent cases of ESP outside the laboratory are not what they seem—that is, we must reject ESP completely—or we must recognize that an extensive revision of physics and physiology is being called for . . . It is not inconceivable that telepathy exists.

[My master's thesis, "Telepathic Information Transfer in Humans of Emotional Data," is reproduced as an appendix in my previous book, *Inner Spaces: Parapsychological Explorations of the Mind,* and was also published in the *Journal of Psychology.*]

Psychic phenomena have been reported since antiquity from all over our planet. They include such common experiences as the feeling of being stared at behind one's back or from a distance, feeling guidance from intuitive gut feelings, premonitions about what is yet to transpire, and near-death experiences. The frequent, but not scientifically understood, medical phenomena of the placebo effect are also a commonplace example of the power of mind over body.

The major categories of psi phenomena researched by parapsychologists include *telepathy* (the awareness of other people's thoughts and feelings); *precognition* (knowledge of future events); *clairvoyance/remote viewing* (obtaining information about objects and events beyond the range of the physical senses); and *psychokinesis* (influencing physical objects from a distance).

Parapsychology has a long history in the West, extending back more than a century with the establishment, by a bold group of leading thinkers and scientists, of the British Society for Psychical Research in 1882.

Despite skeptical suppression by the scientific establishment, both the Soviet Union and American militaries were sufficiently convinced of the apparent reality of psi phenomena to conduct their own research in their attempts to gain strategic advantage over each other. Project

Stargate, for example, was the code name for a secret US military psi research project with the prestigious think tank SRI International, headed by physicist Hal Puthoff. The research results were sufficiently encouraging for it to be continued under various government agencies for about twenty-five years. It focused mostly on "remote viewing," or the ability to psychically "see" events and sites and access other potentially important information from a great distance away. This controversial program was reputed to have provided actionable intelligence for several hundred missions.

Edgar Mitchell, late lunar astronaut and sixth man to walk on the moon, had a profound mystical experience in space that led to his establishment of the Institute of Noetic Sciences (IONS) to conduct psi research. (Mitchell, like many of the other astronauts, experienced the "Overview Effect." This is the experience of seeing the Earth from outer space as a unique and unitary whole, with a resulting mystical shift in attitude about what makes up reality. It's an epiphany about the interconnectedness of everything and the central role of consciousness.) Nearly half a century later, IONS is where the highest quality leading-edge research in this field is being conducted, currently under the leadership of their brilliant chief scientist, Dean Radin.

Dean Radin recently stated that the accumulated experimental evidence in parapsychology for various categories of psi phenomena has surpassed odds of more than one billion to one against simple chance explanations.

Another IONS-based venture (from the former

Princeton University Engineering Anomalies Research Lab) is the Global Consciousness Project directed by Roger Nelson. It's a multidisciplinary international collaboration of scientists and engineers who collect data continuously from a global network of physical random number generators, located in up to seventy host sites around the world at any given time. Their research for more than two decades is proving that large-scale group consciousness can affect the physical world. They track the impact of the simultaneous focused attention of millions of people worldwide during major global events (that engage and synchronize their feelings) on the random physical measurement devices. This research alone has yielded results exceeding the seven-sigma level of odds against chance of more than one trillion to one.

Similarly, the Global Coherence Initiative, launched in 2008 by the HeartMath Institute, researches how compassionate living from a state of heart coherence can positively affect and lift the vibration of those around us and of the entire planet. They research the interaction between internationally located human participants and Earth's magnetic fields by using a worldwide network of ultrasensitive magnetometers. The Global Coherence Initiative's data have revealed a strong correspondence between the former and the basic electromagnetic field of the human heart, as monitored by heart rate variability (HRV). So the collective feelings and intentions of participants in a meditative-like state can impact Earth's magnetic fields.

Ironically, the generally accepted fundamental concepts in leading-edge physics about the nature of our reality (i.e., that quantum mechanics is nonlocal and observer-dependent, as discussed in chapter 5) depend on the same type of seemingly subjective and physically impossible explanatory conceptions as psi phenomena. Moreover, the collective knowledge basis for psi is stronger than that of the more conventional materialistic fields of knowledge.

> *That humankind has fallen into the insanity of consensus trance, and lost touch with our true possibilities and functions, is a tragedy.*
>
> —Charles Tart, psychologist and parapsychologist

One of the most exciting recent breaches of materialistic scientism, inspired by the discoveries in parapsychology and quantum physics, was the establishment in 2017 of the Academy for the Advancement of Postmaterialistic Sciences. It was formed by leading-edge international scientists bravely challenging the pseudoreligion of scientism and its dogmatic exclusion of the true underlying sources of our experiences and the interconnected nature of our relationship with our world (sort of reminiscent of the fabled parable by Danish author Hans Christian Andersen "The Emperor's New Clothes)."

In 2019, following widespread consultation with ninety advisers representing thirty universities worldwide, there was a similar wake-up call to the scientific establishment— the publication of the Galileo Commission Report by the international, UK-based Scientific and Medical Network.

Hmmm . . . perhaps, as expressed in the words generally attributed to the visionary Jesuit priest and philosopher Pierre Teilhard de Chardin, *"We are not human beings having a spiritual experience. We are spiritual beings having a human experience."*

How do I know the way of all things at the Beginning? By what is within me.

—Tao Te Ching, Chinese classic Taoist text, sixth-century BC

*I searched for God and found only myself.
I searched for myself and found only God.*

—Rumi, thirteenth-century Sufi mystic

07

Historical Spiritual
Teachings About
the Primacy of
Consciousness

In prescientific times it was generally believed that various gods controlled both our personal fate and that of the external world (quite the opposite of the modern obsession with materialism). They were also believed to naturally possess supernatural knowledge and powers (because they were gods). Ironically, these are also the very same types of abilities and phenomena that the materialistic-reductionist paradigm model of reality denies as being possible (even for gods).

Back then and through today, ordinary people in a variety of circumstances located all over Earth occasionally have mystical and shamanistic experiences of nonordinary reality. These experiences feel more real than ordinary material reality and are powerfully life changing.

Such mystical occurrences are generally considered to be ineffable. For while words are useful in communicating familiar or shared experiences, they are frustratingly inadequate when attempting to explain radically different experiences.

Nevertheless, the experiencers of such phenomena do characteristically report a sense of being in the "eternal now" and connecting with the Oneness of the Allness. (As did some astronauts, like Edgar Mitchell, with the Overview Effect.) It's a transformative experience, as they come to a deep understanding that the universe is participatory consciousness.

As the Indian yogi Sri Aurobindo taught, "This universe is a gradation of planes of consciousness."

Nineteenth-century Canadian psychiatrist R.M. Bucke wrote about his personal mystical experience of "cosmic consciousness." He experienced the cosmos not as dead matter but as a living presence, and he had the realization that "the foundation principle of the world is what we call love" (because it *connects* us all).

> *Whoever does not love does not know God, because God is love.*
>
> —John 4:8

Over time, the mystical experiences and accumulated teachings about them became codified differently in the various religions. However, the actual mystical experiences underlying the religious beliefs were de-emphasized and discouraged. And all too frequently, the developed doctrines became enshrined as absolute truth—not to be questioned because of the risk of being accused of heresy.

Religions in various forms extend back to the very dawn of history. There are currently over four thousand active religions in the world. In Christianity alone, it's been estimated that there are over forty thousand denominations globally.

So many confusing messages and interpretations. And this is further compounded by the fact that most religions and denominations claim to be the one and only true path.

So how do you see the forest from the trees? As the scientist and philosopher Alfred Korzybski remarked, "The map is not the territory." In other words, the map of reality is not the same as the actual reality. It's a matter of shifting how you think about things—to not be overly rigid and invested.

> *Children must be taught how to think,*
> *not what to think.*
>
> —Margaret Mead, cultural anthropologist

Aldous Huxley rose above his own religious heritage
to research the commonalities in the major world religions, which he detailed in his book *The Perennial Philosophy*.
(As in modern signal detection theory, he distinguished the
signal from the noise by seeking the common elements in
all the major expressions of the teachings. Essentially, by
identifying the same fundamental concepts and guidelines
in different religious writings, he increased the probability
of their accuracy from an original source.)

What are the commonalities in the mystical core of the
major world religions?

- Reality is multidimensional, and what we commonly experience is only a superficial portion of
  the greater whole.
- The underlying reality for all of existence is
  universal consciousness.
- Love is the organizing principle of the universe.
- Our ego (our egoic sense of self) blocks our
  connection with the deeper level of ultimate reality
  of which we are but an extension, and therefore
  needs to be transcended.

Hence the wisdom of the Golden Rule to "do unto
others as you would have them do unto you"—a maxim
reflecting our interconnectedness that is found in many

of the world religions, including Buddhism, Christianity, Confucianism, Hinduism, Islam, Judaism, and Taoism.

Similarly, it explains the logic of the religious notions of sin and karma (e.g., the biblical proverb "You reap what you sow"), since we're all ultimately *connected*.

The Buddha, or Awakened One, realized that suffering was self-created by the illusion of the egoic self and the sense of separation. He then dedicated himself to teaching others how to wake up to find true freedom. He realized that we become caught up in our limited interpretations of reality and constrained by our emotional attachments, which condition our actions and so create unnecessary suffering for ourselves.

The major religions teach us about the primacy of consciousness—and that we have a natural birthright for self-transcendence, which allows us to connect with our deeper spiritual essence.

But how do you wake up to step out of the hypnotic virtual drama to be who you really are, and could be?

The Christian teaching is "Ye must be like a child again to enter the kingdom of heaven."

In Zen Buddhism, *Shoshin* means *beginner's mind*—having an attitude of openness with a lack of preconceptions.

In the *Tao*, written by Lao Tzu in China about twenty-five hundred years ago, the very first line is, "The Tao that can be told is not the eternal Tao." In other words, ultimate reality cannot be fully understood intellectually; it can only be experienced through the silent stillness deep within you.

And then there's the Bible, Psalm 46:10: "Be still and know that I am God."

As you will learn from the exercises in chapters 9 and 10 and additionally in the appendix, the essential formula for real discovery is already within you.

In my previous book, *Inner Spaces*, I speculated that because of the convergent descriptions of *The Perennial Philosophy* in the major religions and the discoveries of the modern sciences, perhaps it's possible to *prove* the case for an empirical theology (rather than rely on blind faith).

Where there is no Vision,
the people perish.

—Proverbs 29:18

The future is not there waiting for us.
We create it by the power of imagination.

—Vilayat Inayat Khan, leader of the Sufi Order International

08

How Reality Works

As you have learned in the preceding chapters from the ancient wisdom traditions and modern scientific discoveries:

- What seems like reality is not what reality actually is.
- Our physical brains are not the source of our consciousness.
- Our individual perceptions are not caused by an independently existing physical reality "out there."
- You are not who you think you are.
- The only thing you can personally know for certain at this moment is that you are experiencing awareness.
- The real basis for the major scientific breakthroughs and inventions is from *internally sourced* intuition and imagination (rather than the result of trial-and-error experimentation).
- Everything is connected, and we live in a *participatory universe*.

The evidence-based and logical conclusion, based both on extensive subjective mystical experiences and scientific findings, is that the popularly accepted materialistic-reductionist model of reality is wrong.

Let us be guided by the wisdom of the Principle of Parsimony, or Occam's Razor. It makes sense to follow the evidence and seek the most obvious explanation rather than rely on untested and theoretical assumptions about an external and material world.

The reality is that our existence and our apparent external world are manifestations of an underlying universal field of consciousness.

If you accept the factual and multifaceted evidence for the primacy of consciousness and the conclusions of many of our wisest and most compassionate voices, then you might wonder—how and why do we figure in all of this?

Be easy on yourself; it's quite a stretch for your finite mind to comprehend infinite consciousness (the source of all that was, is, and will be). It's more comfortable to understand things in terms of objects or circumstances with which we are familiar.

By way of metaphor, picture the infinite field of consciousness (the *Universal Mind*) like the ocean. It has great and mysterious depth and extends with great breadth into the far beyond. On the surface are fluctuating waves, some small ripples, others enormous. The waves eventually change shape and size; some new ones appear, and old ones disappear. But all of them are temporary and superficial extensions of the same underlying ocean. They all come from a common base—so despite their differences, they're all *connected* (what the mystics call the Oneness of the Allness).

Now consider the possibility that we ourselves are like the temporary wave *extensions* of an underlying infinite cosmic sea of consciousness. The waves are one with the underlying ocean from which they emerge and descend, but the ocean is much greater than the superficial waves. (Perhaps this explains Jesus's seemingly contradictory statements: John 10:30, "I and the Father are one" and John 14:28, "The Father is greater than I.")

This conception also fits the description in the *Amritbindu Upanishad*, an ancient Vedic text, *that in whom reside all beings and who resides in all beings.*

As I explained in *Inner Spaces*, our truer nature is like that of "amphibious beings," living parts of their lives in two completely different environments. In our case, we obviously experience ourselves as an independent egoic self among other sentient beings in our shared consensual reality. And yet we can also alter our states of consciousness by various means, such as Shamanic rituals, meditation, and psychedelic substances, to potentially experience non-duality—being united with the underlying sentient oneness of it all. (*Nonduality*—literally *not-two*, is the metaphysical concept common to Taoism, Hinduism, Buddhism, Judaism, Christianity, and Islam, that refers to the essential oneness of life.)

In *Inner Spaces*, I used another metaphoric illustration: *The similarity of physics to ancient mysticism is like a Möbius strip which by its nature loops back on itself.* The illusion of there being two different sides only appears as such when viewed partially from one of the optional perspectives. Similarly, this serves as an analogy for the complementary relationship between our subjective awareness and the outer world, which seem separate but are actually connected and interdependent.

Einstein explained that *time and space are modes by which we think and not conditions in which we live.* A Universal Mind doesn't have to have had a beginning, a time before its own existence (just as with the Judeo-Christian-Muslim conceptions of God as the eternal and creator).

Consciousness experiences itself as both subject and object and isn't bound by its own creations. However, there's an existential need for such an omniscient and omnipotent Universal Mind to have things to be aware of. Consciousness is *awareness*, but in order to be aware there must be something to be aware of. There is also a need for new and interesting things—one is a lonely number—which implies change and unexpected occurrences, so things evolve into increasing diversity and complexity. (Perhaps the Universal Mind needs to dream us up for its own entertainment and expansion—somewhat like when we engage in daydreaming.)

Perhaps our real nature as apparent individuals in our consensual reality is analogous to the dissociated alters in multiple personality disorder (now termed in psychiatry as dissociative identity disorder).

We are existing in a participatory universe. We are the created and the creator. And the underlying field of consciousness exists and manifests through our own experiences in the playground of our everyday lives.

Remember, physical reality is mere waves of probability imagined and observed into form.

There are reasons why our real source and identity is not more broadly known (or experienced). Human minds have a *fail-safe* to protect the virtual reality cover from being exposed. This fail-safe is so convincing that we cannot easily wake up from it to realize the truer nature of our existence. One aspect of this is the emotionally dominated character of the egoic self, which is preoccupied with protecting and inflating its short-term interests. Another from parapsychological research is "psi resistance." This refers both to the irrational and unethical fearful behavior of mainstream scientists and others to suppress such research and also the challenging elusiveness of being able to research psi phenomena (like trying to catch up with your own shadow).

Alan Watts was an eminent British philosopher who specialized in interpreting the teachings of Asian religions for the Western world. In *The Book: On the Taboo Against Knowing Who You Are*, he describes this veiling of reality as a metaphorical game of hide and seek. God (or the Universal Mind) shapeshifts into being you and I and all the people, animals, plants, and stars so It can have entertaining adventures. It's done so well that it's hard to remember where and how It hid itself. Watts goes on to provide the mythical explanation of your relationship to the greater reality from the ancient Vedantic philosophy of India: despite your amnesia, the world is looking at itself through your eyes. We are providing another way for the universe to become conscious of itself.

| *The kingdom of God is within you.*

—Luke 17:21

And as you will soon learn—the only way out, is In!

> **Important—Our virtual reality is a full-immersion experience—it feels very real. Pain hurts; we can bleed and seriously harm others. In this plane of reality, it's wise to also take care of our physical bodies and social needs while being compassionate of the others around us.**

Entrapment by the Ego and the Dark Side

That which is aware, is not the same as that of which it is aware (just as the eye cannot see itself). And you have learned that you are not who you think you are.

Rather, everything you perceive through your senses is like a simulation that immerses you into a virtual reality. Once you learn to identify your egoic self with the simulation, you become emotionally entrapped in it. As the erudite physician and New Age author Deepak Chopra tweeted, "Don't confuse yourself with your selfie."

Ram Dass, American psychologist, psychedelic drug pioneer, and guru, also cautions about the need for humility in attempting to escape from the egoic self: "If you think you're enlightened, go spend a week with your family."

The Dalai Lama has been particularly concerned with our vulnerability to destructive emotions. According to Buddhist philosophy, all personal unhappiness and interpersonal conflict are the result of the "three poisonous emotions": greed, ignorance, and hatred. Look at our world now—all three poisons are dominating our choices and actions, resulting in current existential crises. The antidote is to learn to develop emotional self-regulation and to be more compassionately focused on the needs of others (love of others, instead of love of power).

Ironically, the *illusion of duality and separation* can feel most painfully real in our romantic relationships. In the beginning of such relationships, there's a spark, a sense of excitement, and an intoxicating connection between the eyes. Initially, it's like gazing through a magical mirror and falling in love with the mutual beingness on the other side. But the connection, the warmth and the joy, is lost when the relationship degenerates back into two separate selves butting heads. And although we want to continue to feel deeply connected, we're very challenged by our filters from two bodies with different personalities and preferences, so the relationship commonly deteriorates into unsatisfying ego competition versus soul connection (i.e., from *we* to *me*).

> *Love and compassion are necessities, not luxuries. Without them, humanity cannot survive.*
>
> —Dalai Lama

There are also cautions from wisdom traditions, such as the Kabbala and Raja yoga, about being emotionally distracted by fantastical psychic experiences from the main goal of transcending the egoic self–level of individual consciousness. (There is also the dangerous risk of becoming insane without proper preparation and guidance—as is true sometimes with psychedelic chemicals.)

You need to understand the deceptiveness and power of your own egoic self in order to become liberated from its distortion and constraints.

Fortunately, we're not fated to be imprisoned by our current experiences. You need to *let go* of the illusion of being an isolated individual entity. Instead, choose to embrace the reality of our shared humanity as part of the Universal Mind. This means evolving from a scarcity and competitive mindset to a sustainable and collaborative global mindset. Despite our several billion stories, we're all united in this dimension of life. And like it or not, our fates are entwined. As modern events illustrate, pollution or infection in one country ultimately affects the entire planet.

Recall the universal wisdom teaching: love is the organizing principle of the universe. Love is not just an emotion; rather, it's deep *connection*—like a communion of souls—as it takes us to the underlying spiritual level.

> *Imagine how our culture, how our lives, will change when we begin valuing go-givers as much as we value go-getters.*
>
> —Arianna Huffington, author

Imagine humankind transformed universally by simply accepting the guidance of the Golden Rule.

Maybe then we'll be able to experience the divinity within all of us.

> *In the faces of men and women, I see God.*
>
> —Walt Whitman

Imagination Is the Source of All Possibilities!

Everything that's been created throughout the history of humankind began by simply *imagining* some desired possibility and then discovering ways to manifest it into the outer material world. (Examples include imagining heavier -than-air flight with airplanes, instantaneous communication over great distances with cell phones, and traveling to the moon with rockets.)

Even our conventional human experiences are proof that *thoughts can become things.*

When you begin to awaken to the dreamlike nature of the universe, you come to realize that the egoic self, which you've been imagining to be who you are, is itself a character being dreamed up by a deeper Self. While you can't stop dreaming because it's the nature of reality, you can soon learn to awaken inside the dream and then intentionally redirect it.

Ram Dass used the colorful concept of central casting to explain how we exist in relation, and only in relation, to others. Simply put: we're all just characters in each other's dreams with our roles as part of the acting cast in a grand play. Perhaps Shakespeare, famed English playwright, was deeply insightful when he wrote:

> All the world's a stage,
> And all the men and women merely players;
> They have their exits and their entrances;
> And one man in his time plays many parts...

Now is a critical time to use our collective power to dream up a better world for our shared-dream reality.

A good start for a better direction would be to heed the words of the popular lyrics written by Hal David in 1965: "What the World Needs Now Is Love."

If you believe, you will receive whatever you ask for in prayer.

—Matthew 21:22

Whatever dream you hold about reality, the universe will prove you right.

—Alberto Villoldo, psychologist and medical anthropologist

09

How to Envision and Navigate Alternative Realities

In modern IT terms, you're learning the source code to the underlying algorithm by which the Universal Mind manifests our external material reality.

In the simpler and wise words of American motivational author Napoleon Hill, the formula for a more desirable future is "Whatever the mind can conceive and believe, it can achieve." The practice and implementation of this concept, however, are not so simple. You first need to risk your sanity by opening your mind, and develop strong self-discipline as well.

Everything depends on your level of consciousness—because everything is a level of consciousness in the manifestations from the Universal Mind.

Preparing the Way

Just as the ocean is turbulent on the surface but calmer below, so a level of calmness and clarity is available when you detach from your egoic self and let go of all concerns.

You first need to learn to slow down your ever-busy monkey mind to open a portal of access to the deeper structures of reality.

The *here and now* is the necessary state to access the truer reality (as your mind has to be here to enable what you intend). The now is your point of power.

Ironically, if you want to be fully present in the here and now, you have to stop trying so much for your future concerns (similar to the Taoist concept of effortless action— *Wu wei*, or not doing). It's about letting go, not brute willpower. Trust the universe—your inner spaciousness. *The Force is within you!*

The practice of modifying the pattern of habitual breathing is common among the various types of meditation and spiritual traditions. Basically, breathing more slowly enables you to *lengthen the space between your thoughts* and then experience the deep inner spaciousness of the field of infinite possibilities. Physiologically, this simple change has real and beneficial effects for both mind and body. The deeper and slower breathing pattern increases the tone of the vagus nerve, which calms down the brain. (It's also the fastest way to down-regulate the overly stressed nervous system.)

You can bring your sense of self to your awareness by simply closing your eyes and taking a few slow and deeper breaths while focusing on the space between your outer ears. (In Sanskrit this space is termed *Chidakasha*, or the mind space.)

Meditation is the ultimate brain hack to access non-local consciousness beyond the illusion of separateness. It's always available to you as an option, wherever you are and whatever your situation. It can be as simple as taking breaks to focus mindfully on your breath. (See the appendix for several of my meditation techniques.)

Applying the Magic: Manifesting

Once you have learned to quiet your mind by being a non-attached observer of your thoughts and feelings (similar to observing how clouds eventually pass through the sky overhead), then you will be ready to work with the plasticity of reality.

Intention is the first key factor. You must first become clear about your goal so you can focus on it with what Buddhists term *one-pointedness of mind*. It's then necessary to learn to sustain your focus on your intention, as it's the force behind everything. This is sort of like a space rocket that must reach escape velocity and continue operating until the craft clears the gravitational field of Earth; otherwise, it will simply fly up and then fall right back down. This is similar to the example mentioned earlier about *striking beyond* the wooden board in karate and taekwondo. You need to learn to focus and sustain your intention despite how you feel and remain nonattached to any distractions. (Meditation is very helpful training for cultivating such one-pointed intention.)

Since where attention goes, energy flows, what we attend to grows in our life (for good or for bad). Unfortunately, most people habitually sabotage themselves by focusing more on what they don't want in their lives rather than on what they do want.

Strengthen your dream for your desired future by focusing on what you desire with a possibility-thinking mindset, instead of disempowering yourself by thinking about the possible obstacles along the path and the longshot odds against succeeding. (As the Shamans teach, *choose to live fearlessly within your sacred dream.*)

Imagination is the second key factor. Since, as you've learned, we're relatively dreamed up by the Universal Mind, your power of imagination is really the way to reshape your future. This involves working with *imaginal thinking* rather than conventional thinking or willpower. (For most people, visualization is the medium for eliciting and applying this latent power. However, in the martial arts of tai chi, aikido, and Systema and the laying-on-of-hands treatment technique of therapeutic touch, the medium is bodily sensations such as warmth and tingling.)

Allow yourself to imagine a vivid vision for your own desired future—it can change the trajectory of the rest of your life. This vision becomes both a map and a booster for your spirit to reprogram your own future reality.

Open your mind to richly envision what it is that you desire to manifest in your future, and then hold it in your consciousness with an attitude of expectation. Your expectation becomes a magnetic-like attractive force that will draw opportunities and synchronicities to you along your path.

> *Ask, and it will be given you.*
> *Seek, and you will find.*
>
> —Matthew 7:7

This is applying your capacity for *inside-out thinking*—the basis for the Shamanic practice of *dreaming the world into being*.

At this juncture, your rational mind might be skeptical and dismiss this as mere wishful thinking (which in psychiatry is pathologized as "magical thinking"). Remember that the previous chapters explained and revealed the truer evidence-based reality that this is all solidly based on. There are many current illustrative examples of its power. The common medical placebo effect is literally mind over matter. The Reverend Martin Luther King's visionary "I Have a Dream" speech for racial liberation changed an entire nation. Elon Musk, visionary eccentric business magnate, industrial designer, and engineer, is now one of the greatest entrepreneurs in the world and pioneer in multiple technologies in extremely diverse industries—from the Tesla electric-powered automobile and recyclable SpaceX rockets to Hyperloop-based high-speed intercity transit systems, SolarCity for sustainable energy, and Neuralink brain-computer implants.

Belief is the third key factor, as revealed in the biblical quote from Matthew 21:22 about the need to believe to receive and Napoleon Hill's simple formula. You need to invest your belief in what you are envisioning in your imagination *as if* it is already real, so that you then can *manifest* it (because it's about doing, not just trying). This is the basis of the placebo effect—wherein expectation results in the manifestation of mental and bodily changes—as well as how young children in martial arts learn to painlessly smash through solid wooden boards.

The clearer your vision, the deeper your openness to the intuitive wisdom and power within, and the more unshakable your resolve, the greater the odds in your favor. (Such is also the underlying source of charisma, which draws and inspires others.)

However, it's important to remember what you learned in the previous chapter about the Universal Mind and the intrinsically capricious design of its extended consciousness into the sentient universe. It has built-in elements of complexity and unpredictability in this level of reality. So just because you wish to achieve something doesn't mean that you can simply have or attain it. What you can learn to achieve is the ability to influence the probabilities toward the *manifestations* of your goals.

Discovery consists of looking at the same thing as everyone else and thinking something different.

—Albert Szent-Györgyi, chemist, Nobel laureate

Change the story and you change perception; change perception and you change the world.

—Jean Houston, psychologist and visionary

10

Stretch Your Mind to Shift Reality

You will now learn some introductory-level exercises and practices to shift reality.

> **NOTE:** For your safety and well-being, do not attempt these exercises if you have a mental disorder or are under the influence of mind-altering psychedelic drugs (before first consulting your trusted mental health care provider).

Exploring the Wisdom of the Ancient Oracle of Delphi's Call to Know Thyself

Let's begin to explore beyond the game show reality of the material realm.

Reflect deeply on each of the following questions:

What is my *felt sense* of my own self? (Or more simply, how do I experience being me?)

Is it the sum of my history, jobs, possessions, and accomplishments, or is that about my story but not me—who I actually am (and could yet be)?

It's not my body, because am I not that which is aware of the sensations from my body?

It's not my thoughts, because am I not the thinker of my thoughts?

It's not my feelings, because am I not the experiencer of my feelings?

Where am I, as I'm not out there?

What am I, if not the *awareness* of being aware?

This exercise enables you to experience what spiritual teacher and author Eckhart Tolle describes: "The beginning of spiritual awakening is the realization that you are not the voice in your head but the one who is aware of the voice. You are the awareness behind your thoughts. As this realization grows, you begin to derive your sense of identity increasingly from the space of awareness rather than from the narratives in your mind."

Thinking Out of the Box

Recall from the first chapter that we're programmed by our experiences to see reality through different lenses. Our beliefs are like filters, blinding us to how others might see and value things very differently.
Let's begin with a simple thought exercise.

What's the shortest distance between two dots on a sheet of paper?
A straight line—right? (After all, that is the literal dictionary definition of "straight line.")
Wrong!

Because the shortest distance between the two dots is when the paper is folded in space so that the dots overlap each other.

By learning to use additional dimensions, such as enabling the folding of space, apparent physical distance becomes but an illusion and is no longer a restricting barrier.

And there are many other dimensions.

Remember: things are not as they seem!

Centering in the Here and Now

The now is your point of power. However, in this era of information overload, "fake news," and the weaponized social engineering that addicts us to watching our screens, it's not so easy to be in control of your own attention.

Just like batteries, our attention has a limited capacity. Using smartphones causes a kind of "inattentional blindness" in which we can see things but not actually perceive them, because of our inability to process the additional visual information. (Several studies have also shown smartphone distraction to be as much of an impairment as alcohol intoxication while driving an automobile.)

Our growing addiction to our display screens robs us of our ability to be fully present in our own lives. Psychologists have discovered measurable decreases in the most important of our defining human abilities for memory, reflective reasoning, empathy, and creativity. Ironically, and perhaps insanely, we are making IT devices more complex and intelligent, at the cost of reducing our intelligence and our consciousness.

Noted mindfulness researcher and teacher Jon Kabat-Zinn of the Mind and Life Institute advises, "Befriend your own attention." He also advises to let go for a while of the outer world so that you can just drop into yourself. Then you can feel your presence and attend to the basic awareness of simply being aware. Ideally, it's best to strive amidst all your daily life activities to be rooted in the here and now, on purpose, most of the time.

And, as Buddhist wisdom teaches, *nonattachment* is the fundamental way to reduce unnecessary suffering. It's important to learn how to not be so vulnerable to the many distractions. That doesn't mean not caring, but rather accepting the reality of the *impermanence* of the world beyond our control and going with the flow.

The disciplined daily practice of meditation enables you to master your mind—to quiet it down by learning to *let go* so that you can intentionally choose what, if anything, to focus on. [See the appendix for some of my meditation techniques and resources.]

Eventually you can learn to access a level of consciousness more basic than your egoic self-awareness. And it's in that space between your thoughts where the very source of your thoughts emerges.

This is also the source of your inner intuitive wisdom, which can guide you like an inner GPS.

Intuition enables you to access, connect, and process information that others often miss. It's the opposite of rational decision making with its dependency on objective facts, analytics, and step-by-step deliberative thinking. Intuition is fast and feeling-based, while thinking is slow and controlled.

Although intuitions are usually experienced as feelings, they're not simple sensations or emotions. You must learn by experience how to perceive intuition amidst the noise.

Just as the stars are always present and shining above (despite cloudy weather, obscuring smog, and light pollution), so is our potential to disengage from distractions and tune into our intuition.

Trust the universe. Be open to the synchronistic opportunities, people, and resources that can manifest seemingly out of the blue to help you achieve your goals.

Be still and know that I am God.

—Psalm 46:10

Emotional Self-Regulating

When your consciousness is stressed and hijacked by fear or anger, your brain is not able to function in a coherent state (so your mind is neither clear nor wise).

Your egoic self keeps you entrapped in this virtual reality by your emotionally charged interests, such as your fears, familiar habits, relationships, finances, and relative competitive status. But these are not about your core self, just aspects of what you're able to be aware of. They are experiences to process, not to control you.

Everything is connected. Your choices and actions affect other sentient beings and the entire ecosystem that sustains life in this plane of reality.

The Dalai Lama teaches that because of our vulnerability to "destructive emotions," we need to learn to develop emotional self-regulation.

The Cherokee Parable of the Two Wolves

An elder Cherokee is teaching his grandson about life. "A fight is going on inside all of us," he explained to the boy.

"It's a terrible fight between two wolves. One is evil. The other is good. The same fight occurs inside you."

The grandson thought about it for a minute and then asked his grandfather which wolf will win.

The wise elder Cherokee replied, "The one you feed."

This story illustrates our power to choose the trajectory of our own lives and that of the world. We do this by being less into our own egos and emotions and instead more compassionately focused on the needs of others.

Shifting our consciousness out of the self-centric survival mode and into the field of loving connectedness enables deeper access to the realm of the underlying Universal Mind. Hence the popularity of the Buddhist "Loving-Kindness meditation" practice.

You can choose to enjoy the warmth of shared presence in human connection rather than be fearfully guarded and distanced from others. For example, as in the five-thousand-year-old Tantric practice of "soul gazing," you can *connect* more deeply with others by simply looking more openly and softly into their eyes (Research by American psychologist Robert Epstein demonstrated that soft mutual eye-gazing for just a few minutes resulted in loving feelings—even between total strangers.)

Maybe there's something true after all about the proverb "The eyes are the windows of the soul."

Choose to cultivate an optimistic mindset so that you can live in hopefulness and possibility. No matter what your situation, as long as you retain consciousness, you always have choices.

> *Between stimulus and response is a space, and in that space is our freedom to choose.*
>
> —Viktor Frankl, Austrian psychiatrist and Holocaust survivor

Awareness of Being Aware

You have many more choices about what you can be aware of and influence than you realize. Instead of passively experiencing sensations in your body, you can open and modify other portals of perception.

For example, lightly place the palm of one of your hands on one of the cheek areas of your face. Now selectively tune in to feel your hand on your face from both perspectives—your hand feeling your face and your face feeling your hand.

Now for a deeper dive into the nature of your reality. This can be quite powerful, so don't freak yourself out too much. Try it for only about five minutes.

Look at your face in a mirror for several minutes. Look into your own eyes. You of course see yourself. But do you really? *What* is actually seeing the visual image of your face?

As the Hindu sage Shankara explained, "That which is aware cannot be the same as that of which it is aware— The Knower is not the known."

You associate with the image of your face and body, but that is not who you really are.

Imaginal Thinking

As you have learned, imagination is the source of all, so it's important to learn to play and work with it. (Yet that is usually discouraged from an early age in modern schools by the reprimands to "stop daydreaming.") A helpful technique to boost this latent ability is to envision your desired future with the aid of a vision board, which comprises drawings or pictures of what you seek to manifest into your reality.

Attention is our fundamental ability. By choosing to *see* things differently, we can learn to do so.

We attend with our senses to various things in the apparent outer material world. However, this reduces our awareness of other things of possibly greater importance.

You can flip your conventional way of seeing things around you by developing *soft eyes* and learning to perceive *negative space* to better experience the underlying *interconnectedness* of everything.

In soft eyes, instead of focusing on one thing, shift into your peripheral perception to enable you to experience the expansiveness of your fuller field of vision and consciousness.

You can learn to see negative space by focusing on the space between the individual things that unites them all instead of looking at the individual things around you (as in the saying "See the forest for the trees"). This provides you with another way to connect everything around you.

Our images are thoughts, and *thoughts become things*. This is the underlying process of the common placebo effect in medicine. Intentionally imagining the expected changes in the sensations and internal physiological processes of your body can produce such physical effects.

Here's an experiential example of the mind/body effect. Vividly imagine the aroma of a freshly cut lemon, an aroma so strong and pungent you can almost taste it. Notice that eventually you feel more saliva flowing into your mouth (as it would to buffer the acidic juice from an actual lemon).

(On a scientific note—salivation is controlled by the autonomic nervous system, which is considered to be involuntary. Yet in this exercise you can discover and prove the very real power of *imaginal thinking* to enable mind over body.)

Extending Energy

Just as you are an outward extension from the underlying field of consciousness, you can learn to further extend and modify your illusory boundaries by shapeshifting (as you're not simply a skin-encapsulated ego).

Energy flows where attention goes.

Imagine you have the ability to extend the sense of touch awareness in your hands by an inch or so *beyond* your actual skin boundary. Notice how quickly you can develop an extended range of that feeling.

Now learn to feel your own energy field, which extends *beyond* your physical body.

I adapted this procedure from an exercise demonstrated by Bernard Gunther (a pioneering energy work teacher at the Esalen Institute in California):

1. Vigorously rub both palms of your hands back and forth for a couple of minutes until you feel a tingling sensation.
2. Extend both arms out horizontally in front of you.
3. Quickly alternate between opening and closing both your hands for a few minutes.
4. Next bring your hands in closer and hold them at about the level of your chest.
5. Position your hands about two inches apart with the palms facing each other.
6. Feel the space between your hands as you move them farther apart and then closer again a few times. Notice the sensations in your hands, such

as heat, tingling, vibrating, or perhaps a cushi-
ony feeling between them.

7. Practice with a partner. Have them close their
   eyes so they can learn to feel the energy ema-
   nating from your charged-up hands. (Sensitive
   people can distinguish whether you're rotating
   your hands in a clockwise or anticlockwise
   direction when your hands are positioned at a
   distance in front and behind of their abdomen.)

8. Or advance to create a projection of a Qigong
   energy ball between your hands. Imagine with
   each breath that you can *feel* an increasing
   amount of your extended energy.

Lucid Dreaming

> *The feeling that dreams show us the
> real nature of reality is something that's
> shared by many indigenous groups
> around the world.*
>
> —Stanley Krippner, psychologist and eminent parapsychologist

> *In dream consciousness we make things
> happen by wishing them, because we*

are not only the observer of what we experience but also the creator.

—Vilayat Inayat Khan, head of the Sufi Order International

Recall from chapter 1 that many of the spiritual teachers of the world conceptualize us as being asleep and failing to realize that we're just caught up in our dreams. (And that it's the egoic self that you identify with that keeps you emotionally entrapped in this all-embracing virtual illusion.)

Dream programming enables you to develop some control in your dreams, both to avoid entrapments and to access more desirable possibilities.

It enables you to hack into the deeper field of the Universal Mind (sort of like swimming underwater in the underlying cosmic sea of consciousness, as described metaphorically in chapter 8). Then you can employ your dreams as a vehicle for shapeshifting to transform the quality of your everyday waking life (as in the practice of Shamanic journeying to dream the world into being).

Dream yoga for such dream control has been used for more than a thousand years by Tibetan Buddhists to explore beyond the illusory nature of reality and is found in many other indigenous practices worldwide.

In Western psychology, this phenomenon is called *lucid dreaming*. These are dreams in which you become aware that you are in fact experiencing a dream and yet you remain asleep. And, with such awareness, you can then take control to modify, or redirect, the dream.

The hypnagogic state of consciousness occurs in the transitional process of falling asleep; the opposite is the hypnopompic state, when we are in the process of awakening from sleep. These transitional states of consciousness are a bridge-like connection between the conscious and subconscious realms of our minds. The practice of lucid dreaming utilizes this temporary two-way connection, in both directions.

So how can you experience lucid dreaming for yourself?

- Firstly, by knowing, as you do now, of its existence and of the possibility for you to experience it personally.
- Hold the goal of experiencing such a dream in mind as you are settling down to sleep.
- Try to remember while in the midst of ordinary dreams about your *intention* to semi-awaken within the dream so as to be able to then redirect it.
- Train yourself to recall immediately on awakening some aspects of your lucid dream experience (*before* fully reorientating back to the here and now of the external world).
- Choose to bring back a token symbol from the lucid dream state into your waking memory. This can then serve as a shortcut connection, like a key, between your waking and dream worlds, so that you can more easily access and navigate through the different levels of consciousness.

APPENDIX

Meditation: The Essential Guidelines

As stated in Buddhist teachings, "Life is hard and unfair." It's even more so in times like these, when the external world is so crazy and scary. Accordingly, be guided by the ancient wisdom teaching: *The only way out, is In.*

Your monkey mind is constantly jumping all over the place, distracting you from the here and now of actual reality. The result is unnecessary stress—clouding your thinking with needless concerns of the past and baseless worries of what might happen in the future.

By contrast, meditation is basically the practice of paying attention to where you are right now—so that your *mind and body are in the same space at the same time*, with clarity and relaxation.

Meditation enables you to control your mind by exercising control of your concentration—to develop the ability to focus on what really matters.

You can learn to be empowered to be your personal best, rather than continuing to be so heavily influenced by others or external circumstances (or even your own self-defeating habits). Additionally, you can learn how to access the helpful inner resources of your creative and intuitive abilities to live a more satisfying life.

The Basic Technique

Find a relatively quiet environment (where you will not be disturbed by any distractions).

Settle down into a comfortable position (with your back supported and head free) that you can sustain without moving or falling asleep.

Close your eyes to help screen out external distractions.

Realize that your body is always here, right now. Choose to focus on the sensations of your body being supported by the underlying surface—be it the ground, a chair, or a bed. This helps to root you back into the *present moment* from the distractions of your otherwise overly busy mind.

Focus your attention mostly on your breathing, which can serve as your ever-present anchor to help you let go of distractions.

Allow yourself to breathe more deeply—from your belly/abdomen (so it expands outward like a balloon inflating)—and slowly.

Inhale through your nose (keeping your mouth closed).

Exhale through your nose or mouth.

On each inhalation/breath, simply focus on the sensations of breathing in.

When your lungs are full, *pause* for a moment of stillness and deepening.

Then exhale/breathe out more slowly and release any unnecessary tensions and concerns.

When your lungs are empty, pause again for a longer moment of stillness—becoming more aware of the space between your thoughts—feeling the *inner spaciousness* and peace of mind.

Continue this process for fifteen to twenty minutes.

Gradually again become more aware of where you are back in your outer environment. Allow yourself to feel a bit of a smile spreading across your face. And then slowly open your eyes.

Repeat this technique twice daily for ideal benefits.

If bothered by distractions during this process, simply focus even more intently on your breathing (instead of struggling to eliminate distractions). Distractions are an exercise opportunity for you to learn how to not be so attached to them by learning to let them pass through you like the clouds passing through the overhead sky.

When you realize that you've drifted off into distracting thoughts or sensations, gently return your awareness to the here and now—feel your body supported by the underlying surface and the always-present anchor of your breathing.

Shower Meditation

When feeling overwhelmed, focus on what you can control and let go of what you can't.

With the external world in such crisis, it's more important than ever to learn how to be in fuller control of your own mind.

Contrary to the assumptions of multitaskers, you can

only focus properly on one thing at a time. But remember, it's also the nature of our unruly monkey minds to jump all over the place. No surprise, then, that it's a frustrating struggle to calm and empty your mind with conventional meditation techniques.

Imagine a meditation technique that, in contrast, is free, easy, and enjoyable, without requiring any extra time or equipment!

In shower meditation there's only one rule—*No thinking out of the shower*.

Basically, in shower meditation, you focus on your bodily sensations while everything else relatively fades off into the background.

The technique is simplicity itself. Just allow yourself to indulge in the various sensuous aspects of the shower experience. Here's some initial suggestions to get you going:

1. Adjust the temperature so it feels just right.
2. Position the shower spray wherever and how it feels best.
3. Smell the aroma of your shampoo.
4. Feel the texture of the lotion in your hand.
5. Massage it pleasantly into your scalp.
6. Smell the aroma of your soap.
7. Spread the soap like a sensuous massage over your body.
8. Finally, feel the refreshing spray on your face washing away all concerns.

The Tranquility Experience©

This unique soft touch and high-tech audio recording facil-
itates your meditation practice. The accompanying musical
track was performed subconsciously by a professional musi-
cian in the midst of a deep state of hypnotic trance. He was
trained under hypnosis to share his experience of being in
an altered state of consciousness via the language of music.
This specially produced musical background helps entrain
your brain and mind into the optimal state of consciousness for meditation more quickly and comfortably.

Part of the uniqueness of this guided meditation is the
special code word you learn while listening to the recording—
eventually you can regain the state of deep mental quietude
and spaciousness any time you so desire. You simply repeat
the special code word in your mind to reactivate the state.

You can order a copy of this recording as a CD or
download it as an mp3 audio file.

Check out the free sampler:
https://drhowardeisenberg.com/tranquility-experience/

NOTES

PREFACE

Albert Einstein, in James Geary, *Geary's Field Guide to the World's Great Aphorists*.

Goethe, in John Anster, trans., *Faust*.

CHAPTER 1

Oracle of Delphi: According to legend, an inscription at the entrance of the Temple of Apollo at Delphi, in ancient Greece.

Thich Nhat Hanh, *Being Peace*.

Thich Nhat Hanh, *The World We Have Now*.

Stanley Krippner, personal correspondence via email, July 27, 2021.

Barbara Marx Hubbard in Ervin Laszlo and Kingsley Dennis, eds., *The New Science and Spirituality Reader*.

CHAPTER 2

Menas Kafatos, "The Participating Mind in the Quantum Universe, Cosmos and History," *Journal of Natural and Social Philosophy 14*, no. 1 (2018): 40–55.

Sandra Ingerman, *Soul Retrieval: Mending the Fragmented Self*.

CHAPTER 3

Albert Einstein, *Cosmic Religion and Other Opinions and Aphorisms*.

Austin L. Hughes, *The New Atlantis*.

Paul Strathern, *Mendeleyev's Dream: The Quest for the Elements*.

CHAPTER 4

Wilder Penfield, *Mystery of the Mind: A Critical Study of Consciousness and the Human Brain*.

Eccles, Sir John C., *Evolution of the Brain: Creation of the Self*.

Peter Russell, *From Science to God: A Physicist's Journey into the Mystery of Consciousness*.

Robert Woodworth, *Dynamic Psychology*.

CHAPTER 5

Shunryu Suzuki, *Zen Mind, Beginner's Mind*.

New Scientist (February 2020): cover.

John Wheeler in Denis Brian, *The Voice of Genius: Conversations with Nobel Scientists and Other Luminaries*.

David Bohm, *The Undivided Universe: An Ontological Interpretation of Quantum Theory*.

Neil Turok, "The Universe Within: From Quantum to Cosmos," CBC Massey Lectures, Toronto (2012).

James Jeans, *The Mysterious Universe*.

Arthur Eddington, *The Nature of the Physical World*.

Max Planck, cited in Bernardo Kastrup et al., "Coming to Grips with the Implications of Quantum Mechanics," *Scientific American* (May 29, 2019).

CHAPTER 6

Sigmund Freud to Hereward Carrington, letter dated July 24, 1921.

Jessica Utts, "Presidential Address to the American Statistical Association" (2016).

D.O. Hebb, "The Role of Neurological Ideas in Psychiatry," *Journal of Personality* 20 (1951).

D.O. Hebb, *Essay on Mind*.

Charles Tart, *Waking Up*.

CHAPTER 7

Rumi, cited in Sunil Daman, *Jalaluddin Rumi Quotes and Poems on Life, Love and Death*.

Sri Aurobindo, *The Synthesis of Yoga*.

Richard Maurice Bucke, *Cosmic Consciousness*.

Margaret Mead, *Coming of Age in Samoa*.

CHAPTER 8

Pir Vilayat, cited in Larry Chang, *Wisdom for the Soul*.

Albert Einstein, in Dimitri Marianoff and Palma Wayne, *Einstein: An Intimate Study of a Great Man*.

Deepak Chopra, Twitter tweet, Sept. 7, 2016.

Dalai Lama XIV, *The Art of Happiness*.

Arianna Huffington, *Thrive: The Third Metric to Redefining Success and Creating a Life of Well-Being, Wisdom, and Wonder*.

Whitman, Walt, "Song of Myself," *Leaves of Grass*.

William Shakespeare, *As You Like It*.

CHAPTER 9

Alberto Villoldo, *The Heart of the Shaman*.

Napoleon Hill, *Think and Grow Rich*.

CHAPTER 10

Jean Houston, *A Passion for the Possible*.

Albert Szent-Györgyi, cited in Gyorgy Darvas, *Hypersymmetry*.

Eckhart Tolle, Foreword, in Peter Russell, *Letting Go of Nothing*.

Viktor Frankl: This quotation is popularly attributed to Viktor Frankl but is of unknown origin.

Shankara in Rene Guenon, *Man and His Becoming According to the Vedanta*.

Stanley Krippner, Personal correspondence via email, July 27, 2021.

Vilayat Inayat Khan, in David L. Kahn, *Boundless Paradox*.

ONLINE RESOURCES

Academy for the Advancement of Postmaterialist Sciences
https://www.aapsglobal.com

American Society for Psychical Research
http://www.aspr.com

Association for Transpersonal Psychology
www.atpweb.org

Esalen Center for Theory and Research
https://www.esalen.org/ctr-main

Galileo Commission Report
https://galileocommission.org/report/

Global Consciousness Project
https://global-mind.org

Institute of Noetic Sciences (IONS)
https://noetic.org

International Association for Near-Death Studies (NDEs)
https://iands.org

Manifesto for a Post-Materialist Science
https://opensciences.org/about/
manifesto-for-a-post-materialist-science

Mind & Life Institute
https://www.mindandlife.org

Parapsychological Association
https://www.parapsych.org

Psi Encyclopedia
https://psi-encyclopedia.spr.ac.uk

Science and Non-Duality (S.A.N.D.)
https://www.scienceandnonduality.com

Scientific and Medical Network
https://scientificandmedical.net

Searching for Superhumans
https://superhumanexperience.io

Society for Psychical Research
https://www.spr.ac.uk

Society for Scientific Exploration
https://www.scientificexploration.org

Spiritual Emergence Network (SEN)
http://www.spiritualemergence.org

University of Arizona Center for Consciousness Studies
https://consciousness.arizona.edu

University of Virginia, Department of Psychiatry and Neurobehavioral Sciences, Division of Perceptual Studies
https://med.virginia.edu/perceptual-studies/

World Psychiatric Association, Section of Religion, Spirituality and Psychiatry
https://www.wpanet.org/religion-spirituality-and-psychiatry

SUGGESTED READINGS

(In order of suggested reading)

The Present, by Spencer Johnson

The Perennial Philosophy, by Aldous Huxley

The Book, by Alan Watts

I Am That, by Sri Nisargadatta Maharaj

Destructive Emotions, by Daniel Goleman

The Naked Ape, by Desmond Morris

A Short History of Progress, by Ronald Wright

An Inconvenient Truth, by Al Gore

Global Mind Change, Willis Harman

The End of Materialism, by Charles Tart

The Invisible Gorilla, by Christopher Chabris and Daniel Simons

The Master and His Emissary, by Iain McGilchrist

The Structure of Scientific Revolutions, by Thomas Kuhn

The Tao of Physics, by Fritjof Capra

Inner Spaces: Parapsychological Explorations of the Mind, by Howard Eisenberg

The Biology of Belief, by Bruce Lipton

The Brain that Changes Itself, by Norman Doidge

Imagery in Healing: Shamanism and Modern Medicine, by Jeanne Achterberg

How to Change Your Mind, by Michael Pollan

The Stargate Archives, by Edwin May and Sonali Bhatt Marwaha

One Mind: How Our Individual Mind Is Part of a Greater Reality,
by Larry Dossey

Real Magic, by Dean Radin

Galileo Commission Report, by Harald Walach

The Way of the Psychonaut: Encyclopedia for Inner Journeys,
by Stanislav Grof

Alone Together, by Sherry Turkle

INDEX

ABOUT THE AUTHOR

HOWARD EISENBERG, M.Sc. (Psych), M.D., is a medical doctor with additional postgraduate training in psychology and psychiatry. He has been a lecturer at the University of Toronto and an associate professor of Medicine at the University of Vermont. He is also the CEO of the international consultancy Syntrek® Inc.

On a more personal level, he's been on a passionate lifelong quest to discover the true nature of reality.

He was awarded the first postgraduate degree in Canada at McGill University for his highly successful research on Telepathy. He then pioneered the instruction of Parapsychology as a regular credit course at the University of Toronto.

Almost half a century ago, he authored his first trailblazing book, *Inner Spaces: Parapsychological Explorations of the Mind.*